Teen Guide to
FINANCIAL LITERACY

Joe Ferry

ReferencePoint
Press

San Diego, CA

© 2022 ReferencePoint Press, Inc.
Printed in the United States

For more information, contact:
ReferencePoint Press, Inc.
PO Box 27779
San Diego, CA 92198
www.ReferencePointPress.com

LIBRARY OF CONGRESS CATALOGING-IN-PUBLICATION DATA

Names: Ferry, Joe, author.
Title: Teen guide to financial literacy / by Joe Ferry.
Description: San Diego : ReferencePoint Press, 2021. | Includes
    bibliographical references and index.
Identifiers: LCCN 2021009643 (print) | LCCN 2021009644 (ebook) | ISBN
    9781678201746 (library binding) | ISBN 9781678201753 (ebook)
Subjects: LCSH: Finance, Personal--Juvenile literature.
Classification: LCC HG173.8 .F47 2021 (print) | LCC HG173.8 (ebook) | DDC
    332.02400835--dc23
LC record available at https://lccn.loc.gov/2021009643
LC ebook record available at https://lccn.loc.gov/2021009644

Contents

Why You Need to Be Financially Literate

Congratulations! As a teenager, you are in a unique position to determine your financial future. Will it be one of freedom and luxury, or will you live paycheck to paycheck? Will you spend responsibly or drown in debt? Will you be able to afford a nice car, a house, vacations, and nice clothes? Or will you live in your parents' basement until they kick you out? And then what will you do?

How and what you learn about handling money now will go a long way in determining which financial track you will take in life. Financial literacy is generally defined as having the right habits and knowledge about money to lead to financial security and the ability to weather an unexpected emergency expense. The financial website Investopedia says the teenage years are often the time in young people's lives when understanding the value of money, and how to earn it, become important. Teens need to learn how to use credit wisely, save for college, budget for a smartphone (not every parent can be so generous), or purchase their first car. Budding young entrepreneurs may be looking for help to give their business idea a go in the marketplace. Then there's learning to invest and manage one's savings. "Basic personal finance for teens is critical in order to thrive independently as adults,"[1] states an article on the *MintLife* personal finance app blog.

So, what exactly is financial literacy? The US Department of the Treasury's Financial Literacy and Education

Commission defines financial literacy as "the skills, knowledge and tools that equip people to make individual financial decisions and actions to attain their goals."[2] The commission says there are five key components of financial literacy: earn, spend, save and invest, borrow, and protect.

Acquire Money Skills

Think about learning how to manage your money the same way you learned how to read and write. At a very early age—even before you started to walk and talk—you were slowly acquiring the tools you need to communicate. All through elementary school, middle school, and high school, you have been learning more and refining the skills you learned earlier. Hopefully, by the time you graduate, you will be proficient in those basic skills needed for success.

But has anyone taken the time to teach you about handling money—how to make it, how to save it, how to spend it wisely, how to make it work for you? Probably not. According to T. Rowe Price's 2019 Parents, Kids & Money Survey, 75 percent of kids said they wished their parents had taught them more about money. Marketing expert Judy Hoberman says parents think the schools are doing the training and the schools think the parents are doing the training. Consequently, many teens lack a basic understanding of money. "Teens are brought into an environment where you use plastic for most of your big purchases, and if you need cash, you go to a little machine and money comes out,"[3] she says.

A Gloomy Picture

Recent statistics paint a gloomy picture about how people manage their money. In one recent survey, 40 percent of adults reported that they would be unable to cover an unexpected expense of $400 without selling something or borrowing money. That survey was conducted by the Federal Reserve System in 2017. In

Most teens say that they would like their parents to teach them more about handling money. Research also suggests that learning financial literacy concepts in high school can lead to positive financial health outcomes later in life.

a separate survey, done in 2019 by the digital learning company EVERFI, 47 percent of college students reported that they felt less prepared to manage their money than to face any other challenge associated with college.

But there is hope. Research suggests learning financial literacy concepts in high school can lead to positive financial health outcomes later in life. A 2018 study of eighteen- to twenty-two-year-olds by Carly Urban, an associate professor of economics at Montana State University, found that those who were required to take some form of financial literacy in high school had overall better credit scores. Credit scores are used by lenders to determine a borrower's likely ability to repay a loan. Another study by Urban found that students who received financial literacy education were more likely to take out less costly federal loans rather than private loans to pay for college. And while they tended to borrow more money through federal student loans, had to work few hours while in school, had higher college persistence rates, and were more likely to graduate, Urban says.

Without a doubt, you will benefit from learning how to manage your personal finances, especially at a pivotal moment in your life as you begin to think about your future. Learning personal finances and important money skills at an early age will give you lots of opportunities to apply them in real life. If you are already in a habit of budgeting, saving regularly, and spending wisely, think about the head start you have in life.

People who understand how money works can start earning and investing from an early age and avoid lifelong money struggles. If you ask people older than you what their biggest financial regret is, a lot of them will tell you that they wish they had started getting serious about money much earlier than they did. Because doing it only gets harder the older you get. It's a good idea to start now so you don't have that same regret a few decades down the road.

credit score

A numerical value that measures your ability and willingness to repay financial obligations

Chapter One

Earn It, Save It, Spend It

Between time spent on academics, extracurricular activities, and your social life, it might seem like your opportunities to accumulate cash are somewhat limited. But as you get older there will be things you need to buy and things you want to buy. You might even have to help out with your family's living expenses. One thing you will need in order to do any of those things is money. How do you earn it?

The way most teens earn cash is with a part-time job. Maybe you stock shelves at the local supermarket or work the counter at a fast-food joint. Jobs like this not only give you a few bucks, they are also a good way to gain valuable life experience, like learning how to follow instructions, solve problems, develop people skills, and be part of a team. Tracy Morgan, writing in the *TeenLife Blog*, says working as a teen can pay off later in life. "[Working] offers a much wider perspective on life, and mixing with people they might not normally have the opportunity to meet is a great eye-opener to the world around them,"[4] says Morgan.

If you have an entrepreneurial spirit, to earn money you might start a side business that matches your skills and the things you enjoy doing. If you like taking care of kids, for example, you can work as a babysitter. If you love animals, you can walk dogs for your neighbors. If you enjoy being outdoors, you can pull weeds, plant vegetables, grow flowers, and mow lawns. If you can bake great cookies and muffins, you can sell them to raise money.

There are other ways to accumulate cash. Your parents might give you a weekly or monthly allowance for doing chores around the house. You might get gifts of cash from family members for the holidays. Or you might make money by selling stuff you don't want or need anymore.

The bottom line is this: once you have started to generate a steady income, it's time to set some financial goals. This is the first step in creating a personal budget, which is essential to effectively managing your finances. Otherwise, that money you earn will likely burn a hole in your pocket and you'll wonder what happened.

Determining Your Financial Goals

Setting goals is an important part of life. Many experts say your goals should follow the popular SMART acronym in setting goals: **S**pecific, **M**easurable, **A**ttainable, **R**elevant, and **T**ime-bound. *Specific* refers to what exactly you are trying to accomplish. *Measurable* refers to how you'll know whether you're accomplishing that goal. *Attainable* refers to whether your goal is achievable. *Relevant* refers to whether the goal is worthwhile given your circumstances at the time. *Time-bound* refers to setting a deadline for achieving your goal.

By using those five characteristics, you will be able to set goals that are neither too easy nor too difficult, make sure you are staying on track, and know when you have been successful. Here's an example of a SMART goal related to money management: Within the next six months (time-bound), I want to buy a new smartphone (specific) that costs $900 (measurable) by saving $150 a month (achievable) so I can stay in touch with my friends and family (relevant).

Rana Al-fayez, a writer for the website FuturFund, which helps teens understand and manage their money, says setting financial goals will depend on your unique situation and what you are trying to accomplish. But no matter your personal circumstances, goal setting is worthwhile. Says Al-fayez, "Setting realistic financial goals gives you a head start to create your budget. It's important to have something to work toward financially, whether it's paying all of your bills on time every month or saving up for a big purchase."[5]

Separating Needs from Wants

Anyone can spend money. That's easy. It's spending money wisely that is hard. One way to help you spend money wisely is to understand the difference between what you want and what you need. If you're spending more money on your wants than on your needs, that's a problem.

Creating a job for yourself that matches your skills and interests is a good way to earn some money. For example, if you like animals, walking dogs for your neighbors is one way to make money doing something that you enjoy.

How do you know the difference? Try to think of your needs as what you must have now and in the next few months. You probably couldn't live without them. Write down what you need with those costs in one column, and write down what you want and those costs in another column. Ask yourself, "Can I do without these wants?" and "Are there alternatives to my wants?"

Another way of understanding the difference between needs and wants is choosing priorities. In his book *I Want More Pizza*, author Steve Burkholder offers this example of choosing priorities: "You have $20 in your pocket and find a t-shirt you love at your favorite store and it costs $20. But you also wanted to give that $20 to your family to help buy groceries. You choose the groceries and it feels great to help out. As a result, however, you gave up the t-shirt. You prioritized groceries over the t-shirt."[6] In other words, a need was prioritized over a want.

Creating a Personal Budget

Once you've started making money and have identified some goals for your cash, it's time to think about putting together a budget, which is basically a plan for how you will manage your finances. Most financial experts agree that creating and sticking to a personal budget is the most useful tool for achieving your financial goals. "Budgeting is probably the most important financial skill every student needs to learn because it's the cornerstone of financial security and, eventually, success. If you learn how to manage a tight budget while in school, you should be able to master budgeting for the rest of your life,"[7] says Al-fayez.

cash flow

The amount of money coming in and going out

A realistic budget helps you manage your money so you are able to pay for the things you need (and want). Managing your cash flow can be a balancing act. You either need to have enough money coming in to pay for everything or you need to cut back on spending when your cash is limited.

One popular budget plan suggests dividing up monthly after-tax income (also known as net income) and allocating it this way: spend 50 percent on needs, spend 30 percent on wants, and sock away 20 percent in savings. That sounds easy, but it helps to understand what each of those categories represents.

Needs are those bills that you absolutely must pay and are the things necessary for survival. These include rent or mortgage payments, car payments, groceries, insurance, health care, debt payment, and utilities. As a teenager you might not have many of those right now, but they will happen someday.

Wants are all the things you spend money on that are not absolutely essential. This includes dinners and movies out, trendy clothing, tickets to sporting events or concerts, and the latest video game. Anything in the wants bucket is optional. Basically, wants are all those little extras you spend money on that make life more enjoyable and entertaining.

Finally, experts say you should try to allocate 20 percent of your net income—the money left after all deductions—to savings and investments. As a teen, this means putting your money in some sort of bank account. As you get older, you might use a portion of your savings as an investment.

As a teenager, you might think a budget is silly and a waste of time. But even if you don't make a lot of money now, developing and sticking to a budget will help you later in life when you do have more money and more expenses. Budgeting is not just a tool for teenagers or young adults. According to the book *The Millionaire Next Door: The Surprising Secrets of America's Wealthy*, almost 60 percent of millionaires use a budget to manage their money. Most of them probably started long before they had a lot of money. They didn't get rich by spending all their money without a plan.

Failing to Budget

There are several potential downsides for people who don't develop and follow a budget. For one thing, they might have difficulty tracking their goals and understanding whether they are on a successful path. Also, they might make random purchases that they don't really need or want, putting their goals further out of reach. If that happens, they tend to regret not having enough money when they really need it. Often, that means going into debt, which takes time to repay.

Budgets are not meant to be like a starvation diet for spending, according to *Money Management: Control Your Cash Flow*, a publication by the High School Financial Planning Program. In fact, if your budget is too restrictive, you'll never stick with it. So it's best to create one that balances your desire to reach your goals with your desire to be satisfied with the ride, according to the publication.

The first step in creating a personal budget is to track your spending over the course of one month, and then break everything down into categories. How much did you spend for food, for clothing, for entertainment? How much did you put aside for savings? Write it all down so you have a good record. Some people use a simple two-column method: expenses on one side and income on the other. Add the lines in each column to see

Doing some of the grocery shopping for your family can help you develop a sense of financial priority because you must put the needs of your family above things you might want to buy for yourself.

if you are spending more money than you are making. You can do this on a sheet of paper or with a computer spreadsheet or budgeting app.

Figuring Out Your Expenses

Expenses can be classified into three types: fixed, variable, and periodic. The purpose of creating a budget is to make sure you don't spend so much money on variable expenses that there's not enough left to pay for fixed or periodic expenses. When that happens, the bill collector comes calling.

Fixed expenses cost the same every time—usually in the form of a set monthly payment. For instance, this could be monthly payments for a cell phone plan or a car loan. Fixed expenses are easy to plan for because you know how much needs to be paid and when. The downside is that the amount is set by someone else (the cell phone service provider in the case of a cell phone, or a bank in the case of a car loan). That means you can't adjust your payment if money is tight.

Variable expenses are common expenses whose amount is different each time, such as paying for takeout food or a movie. One good thing about variable expenses is that you have control over how much they are. For example, you can change how often you eat out and where you go. So if you're really tight for money, you could stop eating out or skip the movie and save yourself some cash.

Periodic expenses arise occasionally during the year, usually less often than once a month. Prom is a good example of a periodic expense. You know when it is, but how much you spend is up to you. Buying gifts for special occasions such as birthdays, anniversaries, or holidays also falls into the periodic expense category. You'll probably want to set aside a fixed amount each month so you have enough money when it comes time to pay for a periodic expense.

Once you have established a budget, it's a good idea to regularly compare your actual expenses to your monthly budget and

You might be shocked when you get your first paycheck and find out it's not for as much money as you expected. Here's why: taxes. Let's say you work twenty hours in a week and get paid $10 an hour. Your gross pay, meaning before taxes are taken out, is $200. But that's not what you get in your paycheck. Certain deductions are automatically taken out of each paycheck. Federal income tax is deducted, as are state and local taxes in some areas. Money is also deducted for Medicare and Social Security, programs that most people rely on in their later years.

Other amounts may be deducted for uniforms, insurance, or other expenses required for work. After all the deductions are taken from the gross pay, the amount left is the net, also called your take-home pay. This is yours to save, spend, or invest any way you choose.

The good news is that you get to file a tax return each year, usually by April 15, for money you made in the previous year. Unless you make thousands of dollars, chances are you will get back most, if not all, of the money that was taken out of your paycheck.

make adjustments to stick to your plan. This is how your budget will help you achieve your short-term and long-term goals.

Pay Yourself First

Almost all financial experts agree that the first item on the expense side of your budget should be "Pay Yourself First." This means that a portion of every dollar you receive—whether it's from a job, allowance, or a gift—should be set aside. Saving 10 percent of your paycheck (before taxes) is generally a good guideline. For example, if you make ten dollars an hour and work twenty hours a week, take twenty dollars from your paycheck and put it aside.

Remember the goals you set before developing your budget? Paying yourself first provides the money you can use to build your emergency fund or to pay for those periodic expenses. Paying yourself first is relatively painless—if you never really had the money in your pocket, you probably won't miss it. Putting that money aside also means you won't have to go into debt when you have to make a big purchase such as a computer or a car. Creating

When you receive money in the form of a check, you can use a smart phone to deposit it in your bank account. It is a quick and easy way to put the money into your savings right away.

the habit of saving money at an early age is an important first step in managing your finances. Those who begin setting aside money for the future when they are young can start a lifetime of healthy savings. "You brush your teeth twice a day and you don't even think about it because it has become a healthy habit,"[8] says financial planner Echo Huang.

It's never too early or too late to start saving. The only mistake is not starting to save at all. And when you start to save, you need a place to put that money so it's safe but easy to access when you need it.

How Bank Accounts Work

There are two types of accounts most teenagers will need: checking and savings. Many banks offer special versions of these accounts for students; these accounts have no or very low fees. A savings account is generally for money you don't expect to spend for a long time. When someone gives you cash for a special occasion—your birthday, for example—you will fill out a deposit slip and take it to your bank along with the money. Or if they give you a check, you can make a mobile deposit using a smartphone. Consider putting some of these gifts in a savings account.

A checking account (not really a good name since most people don't use paper checks anymore) is where you put money that you will probably spend in the short term to pay your regular expenses. Most checking accounts come with a free debit card that you can use for purchases in person or online. One advantage of a debit card is that you can never spend more money than you have in your account. Each purchase is automatically deducted from your checking account, and you'll get the dreaded "Card Declined" message if you don't have enough money to pay for something. You can also easily keep track of your spending with a debit card so you can stick to your budget.

Earning money, learning to spend it wisely, and saving are the cornerstones of financial literacy. Developing good habits now will pay off in the long run.

Chapter Two

Taking On Debt

Credit is such a positive word. You get credit for doing the right thing. You get extra credit for going beyond what is expected. Nobody loses sleep over getting credit. It feels good just to say the word.

Debt is not such a positive word. A debt is something that has to be paid back. Criminals owe a debt to society. Plenty of people lose sleep over debt. It's a word dripping with gloom and doom.

Yet credit and debt are two sides of the same coin when you are talking about your finances. If someone extends credit to you—a bank, a credit card company, your parents, or even your best friend—it creates a debt that you have to pay back, sometimes at a very high cost. If you do not handle credit correctly, it can create a debt that makes your life miserable for a long time. Having too much debt at an early age can make it difficult, if not impossible, to take major steps in your life like moving out on your own or starting a family. "Debt is dumb. It really is," says financial guru Dave Ramsey. "Debt robs your present and steals from your future. Debt keeps you stuck in a cycle that makes it impossible to build wealth. Debt shoves your goals far off into the distant future. But people in debt sometimes can't see all those things. They're so caught up with being in debt that they can't see a way out."[9]

That being said, credit is a fact of life in our economy. Used wisely, it can be a useful tool for accomplishing your goals in life. Most people cannot afford to pay for everything with cash, so credit (in the form of loans) for big purchases such as houses, vehicles, and education is routine for many people. The important thing about credit is to use it for the right reasons and use it only when you know for a fact that you can pay back your debt according to the terms you agreed to with the lender.

The True Cost of Using a Credit Card

A credit card might seem like you're getting access to free money. Just swipe that little piece of plastic (or insert it into a chip reader) or add its numbers to an online shopping site and get the stuff you want. It sounds simple, but it's not. A credit card represents a loan. You're not using your money to make that purchase— you're using the credit card issuer's money. You have a credit limit that you can borrow, and unless you pay off the full amount each month, you will be charged interest for using that money. The bigger the balance you carry, the more you'll pay in interest.

Let's say you decide you want to buy a new tablet that costs $300 but you haven't had time to save up enough to buy it with cash. Your parents cosigned the application, so you were able to get a credit card in your name. If the credit card company charges you 18 percent interest, you only have to make a minimum payment of $15 a month. It sounds great, right? You just got a brand-new tablet, didn't have to spend any cash out of your pocket, and will only have to pay $15 a month. What a deal!

Hold on a minute. At $15 a month and with an 18 percent interest rate, it will take you twenty-four months to pay off the balance in full. That means you will have paid $359 for the tablet ($300 original cost, plus $59 in interest). And if you happen to accidentally miss a payment, your interest rate will probably go up and you'll be charged a late fee, maybe $25 or more. Does it still seem like a good deal?

Now imagine that you only make the minimum monthly payments and continue to use your credit card for everyday purchases like lunch, clothes, and video games. Pretty soon you rack up a $3,000 balance. With an 18 percent interest rate—and even if you make no more purchases—it will take you nearly twenty-two years to pay off your debt. If you were eighteen when you made your first purchase, you will be forty when you finally pay it off. You also will have paid $4,100 in interest charges during that time, well over the amount you originally spent.

Using Credit Wisely

The lesson you should learn from the above example is pretty clear: pay off your credit card balance in full each month by the due date. That way you won't have to pay interest, and you'll never get hit with a late fee.

Many experts have shared other tips for being smart with credit cards. One of these is to know the card's APR. APR stands for "annual percentage rate" and is the number used to calculate how much extra money you have to pay back. Some credit card issuers use rewards like cash back on each purchase to entice you to use their card. "Ignore the glitz and points and choose the card with the lowest annual percentage rate (APR) and fixed fees,"[10] says Alana Biden, an editor at MoneyGeek.

> **APR**
>
> The annual percentage rate of interest a borrower pays to the lender

Also, she warns to beware of cards that offer a low introductory interest rate—sometimes zero percent—for the first six to twelve months. After that period ends, the interest rate usually shoots up to a high amount.

Another tip from experts is to stick to your budget, not the card credit limit. Spending up to the credit limit could, and often does, go beyond people's budgets. Credit cards make it easy to lose sight of how much money you can actually spend. "The problem with cards is that they can feel like Monopoly money, and result in kids spending more than they would if they had to part with cold, hard cash,"[11] says personal finance expert Beth Kobliner in her book *Make Your Kid a Money Genius (Even If You're Not)*.

Using a credit card to buy items like tablets or computers may sound like a good idea, but it can cause stress when you find that repaying your debt takes up most of your earnings.

Yet another tip from experts is to check your balance weekly. This can be done by downloading the app provided by the credit card company and checking it often to make sure your balance is not creeping up. Just because your credit card has a $1,000 spending limit, for example, doesn't mean you should use every penny. In fact, most experts recommend using only about 30 percent of your available credit to limit the amount of money you have to pay back. So if your limit is $1,000, never let your balance get above $300.

Borrowing Money to Buy a Car

For a lot of teens, buying a car is one of the first experiences with sizable debt. Most teens (and most adults, for that matter) don't have the cash to plunk down at the local dealership and just drive off. Most people, when they buy a car, have to borrow the

The minute you start engaging in business online, the chances of someone stealing your identity and using it to commit fraud skyrocket. Identity theft occurs when an unauthorized party uses your personally identifying information, such as your name, address, Social Security number, or credit card or bank account information to assume your identity in order to commit fraud or other criminal acts. According to a 2020 Identity Fraud Study by Javelin Strategy & Research, which helps its clients make informed decisions in a digital financial world, total cost of identity fraud in the United States reached $16.9 billion in 2019.

While there are no guarantees that your identity will not be stolen, experts recommend several steps you can take to minimize your risk.

- Use different passwords on all your credit card, bank, and phone accounts.
- Never keep passwords, personal identification numbers, or your Social Security card in your wallet or purse.
- Never give out personal information on the phone, through mail, or over the internet unless you know the receiver and have initiated the contact.
- Shred or destroy discarded financial statements.
- Give out your Social Security number only when absolutely necessary.
- Use a secure browser to guard the security of your online transactions.

money—usually from a bank or credit union. That means applying for a loan, either with a cosigner (just like for a credit card) or on your own if you have an acceptable credit score.

A car loan is the same as a credit card in that it comes at a price. You pay interest for the privilege of borrowing the bank's money. However, it is different in that it is for a fixed amount of time (the term), and you make the same payment each month until it is paid off.

Here's an example of how car buying works. After looking at several models, you find a safe, reliable model at a local used car lot that you want to buy. After a bit of negotiation with the salesperson, you agree to buy the car for $11,000. After adding in the sales tax, the vehicle registration fee, and other costs, the total bill is $12,000.

You've been preparing for this day over the past couple of years. A car was one of the goals you set for yourself, and you've managed to put aside 10 percent of your paycheck, allowance, and gifts in a savings account for the past two years so you would have money to put toward buying your car. The $3,000 you managed to save is the down payment. Now, where is the other $9,000 coming from?

Getting the Loan

The bank or credit union where you opened your accounts may offer vehicle financing, so it might be a good idea to start there since you already have a business relationship with them. Or you can use financing offered by the dealership. Either way, there are two important factors when considering a car loan: how much you will pay in interest and how long you have to pay it back.

Let's say your bank offers a 5 percent interest rate on used cars (the rate for new cars is usually lower) and a term of forty-eight months. That means you will have four years to pay back the loan but will have to pay 5 percent of the purchase price ($9,000) in interest. Your monthly payment will be $207, and you will pay a total of $9,949 over the life of the loan ($9,000 purchase price plus $949 in interest).

If that monthly payment fits into your budget and the bank thinks your credit record shows you are willing and able to pay your debt in full, the deal will go through. But that's not the end of your financial responsibility when becoming a vehicle owner. Remember, there are annual registration and inspection fees, insurance, gas, and repairs to think about. Those expenses add up and need to be included in your budget.

Buying a car is often a young person's first experience with sizable debt. Since most people do not have the cash to purchase a car outright, a loan is usually required.

Your Credit Score

As a teenager, when you first apply for a credit card or a loan from a bank, someone will have to cosign for you, probably your parents. The credit card company or the bank issuing the loan will look at your cosigner's credit score to make sure the person has a good history of paying his or her debts on time and in full. Remember, a cosigner is just as responsible as you are for making payments; if you don't do it, the cosigner will have to.

After a while, you will have your own credit score, also known as a FICO score, which is a numerical way to summarize your ability to handle loans and other financial obligations—kind of like the grades you get on your report card. There are three primary companies that keep track of credit scores: TransUnion, Experian, and Equifax. Every time you apply for credit, the lender will check your credit score with one or more of these companies to make sure you are not falling behind on your debts. A credit score of 800 is considered excellent. Below 600 is considered poor.

Making sure your credit score remains as high as possible is essential to managing your finances. "Without a good credit score, you might end up paying much higher interest rates on car loans and mortgages—if you can even get those loans at all," says Debbie Schwartz in an article on the Sallie Mae website. "In some states, your credit score might affect your car insurance premium, and there are some landlords that run credit checks before they'll let you into an apartment."[12]

Your credit score is determined by a combination of payment history and credit utilization. If you miss payments or regularly pay late, that can drag down your score. However, when you pay your credit card bill on time each month, that creates a record of responsible behavior that boosts your score. Using more than 50 percent of your credit limit and carrying a balance each month can also result in a lower score. "Basically, anything you do with

Recovering from a Credit Card Nightmare

By the time Amy Nickson graduated from college, she had accumulated more than $88,000 in debt, including $51,000 on credit cards. The cause: reckless spending habits and failing to make payments. She had no idea what to do about it.

She began by contacting a debt settlement company, which helped her get rid of $16,000 of debt with the highest interest rate. Then she had to tackle the rest of the debt on her own. Nickson began by paying off the smallest balances, then slightly larger ones, and so on. She also committed to making the minimum payments on time for the rest of her debts.

Meanwhile, she created and followed a budget for all expenses, making financial needs a priority and cutting out all financial wants. She also took on a part-time job to increase her income. "I had to transform myself from a spendthrift to a frugal person," she says. "I was determined not to amass further debt."

After three and a half years, Nickson was free of credit card debt. She still has student loans but is paying them off gradually. "Most importantly, I sleep peacefully," she says. "And I no longer worry about calls from creditors."

Amy Nickson, "$88,000 Nightmare," HumbleDollar, December 13, 2017. humbledollar.com your credit card is reported on your credit report, and the information from your report is used in the formula that figures your credit score. Practice good credit habits, and you'll see a better credit score,"[13] says Schwartz.

In a perfect world, no one would incur debt. Everyone would have plenty of cash to buy everything they need or want. But there are certain times in life when taking on debt is unavoidable, such as when you buy a car or go to college. Understanding how to manage debt by not borrowing too much money and paying it back on time is a major lesson in creating a stress-free financial life.

Chapter Three

Paying for College

Not everyone is meant to go to a four-year college. Plenty of successful people graduate from two-year schools, earn industry certifications, attend trade schools for specialized skills, enter the military, or go straight into the workforce. There is no single path to success. Only you can decide which path is right for you.

But if you do plan to attend college, the first question to ponder might be this: how will you pay for it? According to a report from the website EducationData.org, the average cost of college in the United States in 2020 was $35,720 per year. Over four years, with inflation factored in, the total cost could be close to $150,000 or more, since only 39 percent of students graduate on time. These costs sound intimidating, but for many students there is a big difference between cost and what you actually pay to attend college. Scholarships and grants can dramatically reduce your real cost. The College Board, which is best-known for developing tests for incoming college students, also analyzes and reports on college costs. It reports that the average net cost (the average that students and families pay after all scholarship money and grant aid are applied) for the academic year 2018–2019 was $14,880 for in-state students at public four-year colleges and $27,290 at private, non-profit four-year colleges.

Realistically, you and your parents will probably have to dip into your savings to pay for tuition, room and board, and other college-related expenses. The typical family covers 43 percent of college costs that way, according to a

2019 report by Sallie Mae, a corporation that provides loans to college students.

Experts say it pays to be a savvy shopper when it comes to comparing costs from college to college. "Just because one school's sticker price is lower doesn't mean it will be more affordable for you,"[14] says Phil Trout, a college counselor at Minnetonka High School in Minnetonka, Minnesota, and former president of the National Association for College Admission Counseling. For example, says Trout, if a $28,000-a-year school doesn't offer you any aid, and a $60,000-a-year college offers you $40,000 in aid, the school with the higher sticker price is actually more affordable.

College Expenses

There are five main categories of expenses to think about when figuring out how much your college education is really going to cost: tuition and fees, room and board, books and supplies, personal expenses, and transportation. You can control some of these costs to some extent. And when you know how much you'll need for these expenses, it makes it easier to create a college budget.

Tuition is the price you pay for taking classes at your chosen college. For example, a college may charge $300 per credit for an undergraduate course. Most general education courses are worth three or four credits, which means you will pay $900 to $1,200 per course. Typically, college students take three to five courses per semester (twelve to eighteen credits).

Some colleges and universities provide a flat rate for tuition, which covers a minimum and a maximum number of units per semester. "That can work well for a student who is committed to a full schedule of classes each term,"[15] says Ken Clark, a writer for the Balance website.

For example, a college may charge $300 per credit but also offer a flat rate of $4,500 per term for twelve to eighteen credits. A student taking only twelve credits is paying $375 per unit, while

the student taking a full load pays $250 per unit. If you think you can handle the workload, take the maximum number of credits allowed to make the most of your tuition dollars, experts say.

In-State vs. Out-of-State Tuition

Tuition can change according to whether you're an in-state student (a resident of the state in which you are going to school; for example, a Philadelphia resident attending Penn State University) or out-of-state student (a resident of a different state than the one in which you are going to school; for example, a Chicago, Illinois, resident attending Penn State). Generally, you will pay more to attend an out-of-state school since state taxpayers help fund state schools.

One way to reduce the cost of college is to earn college credits while you are still in high school. The fewer college credits you have to pay for, the less you will spend on tuition and fees. There are three primary ways to do this.

Advanced Placement (AP) courses: The College Board offers high school students access to more than thirty Advanced Placement courses in English, science, mathematics, history, world languages, and the arts. Your study in these subjects is followed by an AP exam. Should you score high enough on this exam, you can earn college credits in that subject.

College Level Examination Program (CLEP): There is no course to take, just an exam. If you feel that you have a certain level of knowledge, you can choose from among thirty-three exams in five subject areas. If you pass the CLEP exam, you earn the credit in that subject.

Dual enrollment program: Many high schools allow students to take introductory college-level courses at local community colleges, state universities, and even private universities. Not only can you earn valuable credits, you also get a feel for what it will take to succeed at the college level.

Where you live while attending college can also affect cost. If you attend a school that is close to home and live at home, that can save a lot of money. But if you choose to attend a school that is far enough away from home that commuting is not practical (or if you just want a chance for some independence), you may choose to live on campus. This will add to the cost of college.

Colleges usually offer a variety of dorm options (room) and meal plans (board) to students who live on campus. Most schools offer a variety of meal plans for their on-campus dining hall. These can range from an unlimited dining plan to a set number of prepaid meals. The charges vary depending on what plan you choose.

You might also choose to live off campus in an apartment (either alone or with other students). In that case, you'll have to figure out your own rent and food costs. Many colleges require students to live in campus dormitories during their first year or two. In your junior and senior years, however, you may have the option of living off campus. Clark says:

> Living on-campus isn't usually the cheapest option, but it does offer the convenience of a single predictable cost. There's also the convenience of living close to your classes and among your peers. Living off-campus can be filled with unwelcome surprises such as security deposits, rent costs during summer vacation, flaky roommates, traffic-filled commutes to school, or neighbors who aren't keen on living next to college students.[16]

Books, Supplies, Transportation

The list of expenses goes on. Of course, you'll need books and other materials for each of your classes. The yearly estimate for books and supplies for the average full-time in-state undergraduate student at a four-year public college is about $1,300, according to the College Board. Some students are able to lower these costs by buying used textbooks or renting them.

College students also face other expenses such as laundry, cell phone bills, off-campus meals, and anything else you normally spend money on. Figure out what you spend on these expenses and add that amount to your budget. Don't forget to factor in transportation. Whether you commute to campus or take the occasional trip home, you'll have to pay for gas, tolls, and maybe even airfare. These costs will vary depending on how you travel and how often. You may be able to find student discounts on travel costs. Don't forget to factor in the cost of gas if you own a car.

Meeting College Expenses

While the cost of a higher education can be expensive, experts say it remains financially worth it to go to college. College graduates typically earn more money than workers who have only a high school diploma. According to research by the Federal

Reserve Bank of New York, the average college grad earns at least $30,000 per year more than the average high school grad. Brandon Busteed, president of University Partners and global head of Learn-Work Innovation at Kaplan, a company that provides services to colleges and universities, says there is no better return on investment than a college education. "Long-standing economic analyses have shown that people who earn a bachelor's degree—on average—make considerably more money over their lifetime than those with [only] a high school diploma,"[17] says Busteed.

Unless you come from a wealthy family, excel academically, or are an extraordinary athlete, chances are you are going to need some help paying for college. Maybe a lot of help. Most students and families have to cobble together money from multiple sources, including scholarships, grants, and loans.

Scholarships

Scholarships are generally awarded on the basis of outstanding performance in high school, whether in the classroom or as part of extracurricular activities. Scholarships, unlike student loans, don't have to be paid back. Thousands of scholarships worth millions of dollars each year are available, and many of them go unclaimed. Your high school guidance counselor should be able to help you use an online scholarship search tool to narrow your selection. Tyler Yates, writing on the *Earnest* blog, says the chances of getting scholarships will be greater if you start thinking about what would make you a desirable applicant as early as possible.

Different scholarships will take into account a variety of factors, but students generally set themselves up for success by getting good grades, participating in extracurricular activities, and building relationships with teachers, professors, and other people who can speak favorably on their behalf. "Many scholarships will require a written submission—so don't shirk your writing class-

Getting the news that you have been awarded a scholarship that will help pay for college is something to celebrate.

es," says Yates. "Your skills in writing quickly and efficiently will be useful when completing multiple essays both for your school applications as well as the scholarships."[18]

Grants

Unlike scholarships, which are awarded based on merit, grants are awarded mostly based on financial need, but they can also be based on your chosen field of study. Like scholarships, grants do not have to be repaid. Grants can come from a variety of sources, including federal and state governments, colleges and universities, public and private organizations, and professional associations. The federal government, for example, awards Pell Grants, Federal Supplemental Educational Opportunity Grants (for extreme financial need), and TEACH Grants (for students who agree to take up a teaching position in a high-need field or in schools that serve low-income families). State-funded college grants typically address financial needs of low-income students, as well as

The first step in the college financial aid process is filling out the Free Application for Federal Student Aid (FAFSA) from the federal government. The FAFSA is the key document that is needed to get federal financial aid in the form of a grant, work-study program, student loan, or scholarship. Each year over 13 million students who file the FAFSA get more than $120 billion in grants, work-study, and low-interest loans from the US Department of Education.

Many colleges and state governments use the same documentation to determine your eligibility for additional assistance. Also, it's a good idea to submit your FAFSA as soon as possible because some colleges award money on a first-come, first-served basis. The FAFSA becomes available every October for the following academic year. Even though the federal deadline to submit the FAFSA is June 30 of each year at midnight Central Standard Time, states and colleges have their own requirements and cutoffs for financial aid consideration.

Ben Miller, senior director of postsecondary education at the Center for American Progress, says, "The FAFSA is your ticket into the financial aid arena. Submitting it puts you in the running to receive financial aid including federal grants, work-study opportunities, student loans, and some state and school-based aid."

Quoted in Teddy Nykiel and Anna Helhoski, "How to Pay for College: 8 Expert-Approved Tips," NerdWallet, August 28, 2019. www.nerdwallet.com.

encouraging and supporting women and minority students in their college careers. States also often offer career-specific grants for service, which may be available to students pursuing degrees and careers in high-demand fields such as teaching and nursing.

After you have applied for available federal and state-supported grants, the next place to look for grant help is the private sector. Corporations and professional associations often offer grants for deserving students who are pursuing degrees in fields associated with that business or organization. You can also find grant opportunities through religious organizations and clubs dedicated to community service if you meet specific eligibility requirements. The college or university you choose to attend might offer grants targeted toward certain portions of the population, such as women or minorities, and for students pursuing degrees in specific fields or disciplines.

Work-Study Job

College students can also obtain extra financial help by applying to the federal work-study program, which funds part-time, on-campus jobs for students with financial need. The jobs are varied: you might work in the library, in a lab, or as part of the maintenance staff. Your hours are limited and scheduled so they don't conflict with your academic or extracurricular activities.

A work-study job is valuable because it provides you with some income, work experience, and important connections after you graduate. If you qualify, you'll see "work-study" listed on your financial aid award. However, just because you're eligible for work-study doesn't mean you automatically get that money. You have to find an eligible work-study job on your campus and work enough hours to earn all of the aid you qualify for.

A work-study job is valuable because it provides you with some income and work experience. Showing prospective students around a college is one of many on-campus jobs that students do to earn money.

Federal and Private Loans

Your financial aid package will likely include some loans that are offered by the federal government. Federal loans are attractive for a number of reasons. You don't have to start paying them back until after you graduate. They generally carry a low interest rate and a flexible repayment schedule. Also, they can be forgiven under certain circumstances, depending on where you work after you graduate college. Some public service jobs offer student loan forgiveness.

After all your other options are exhausted—savings, scholarships, grants, a work-study job, and so on—you might need to borrow money from a private lender such as a bank. If you do need to use private student loans, compare your options before you choose a lender. Shop around to find the lender that offers you the lowest interest rate and the most generous borrower protections. Common protections include flexible repayment plans or the option to put your loans in forbearance, a temporary delay in making payments, if you're struggling financially.

forbearance

A temporary delay in the responsibility to repay a debt

Remember that after you graduate, you'll have to pay back any money you borrowed. Many student loans accrue interest while you're in school, which means you'll have to pay back more than you originally borrowed. You can use a student loan calculator to see how much you'll owe later depending on what you borrow now.

accrue

To accumulate over time

Choosing to pursue a college education is a major life decision and should not be taken lightly. Understanding the costs you face, considering your options for reducing them, and putting together a strategic plan as soon as possible so you don't take on an insurmountable mountain of debt are critical steps to your ultimate success.

Chapter Four

Living on Your Own

Most teens dream of the day they can move out on their own, to be free of nagging parents and curfews and other restrictions. "As appealing as this may sound, the freedom of living on your own comes with great responsibility, financial and otherwise. Before you take this bold step, make sure you're fully prepared for what lies ahead,"[19] says personal finance writer Valencia Higuera.

One of the ways you can prepare for living on your own is to start paying your own bills while you're still at home with your parents. Higuera suggests offering to contribute to your family's household grocery expenses, utilities, or internet service provider bills. By assuming responsibilities one at a time while still living at home, you can slowly get used to financial independence, she says.

Getting an Apartment

When you're finally ready and do move out on your own, whether it's right after high school, college, or military service, you have two choices: you can buy or rent a place to live. Unless you're making $50,000 a year and have a rich uncle who leaves you a bundle of cash for a down payment, your first place out on your own will probably be an apartment.

When you look for an apartment, be sure to take note of what is included in the lease terms. A lease is a legal document that spells out the rights and responsibilities of the landlord (the person who owns the apartment) and the lessee (you). "Read your lease. It's long, it's boring, it's filled with rental legalese, but take the time to actually read it," says Alecia Pirulis, content marketing manager for Apartments.com. "Make sure you understand it, and don't be afraid to ask questions about the lease—especially any items you don't understand or want more information about."[20]

The typical apartment lease covers one year and includes the amount of rent to be paid each month and when to pay it. The amount should stay the same for at least the first year of the lease. It can go up after that, perhaps by 3 to 5 percent. Most apartment leases require rent at the beginning of each month, with a five-day grace period before it is considered late. Paying rent on time is a good habit to get into. Late rent payments can have a negative effect on your credit score.

Signing a lease obligates both parties—you as the lessee and the landlord as the lessor—to follow certain rules. For one, it means the landlord can't kick you out before the lease expires (unless you break the rules it lays out), and you can't leave before the lease expires (if you do leave you will still be responsible for paying rent for the whole term. Who wants to pay for something they're not using?).

After the initial twelve-month term expires, most leases then go month to month. The lease will point out how much notice either the landlord or the lessee must give to end the lease. Typically, it's thirty or sixty days. The purpose of giving notice is to allow the landlord enough time to find another tenant to replace you and to give you enough time to find another place if the landlord decides they don't want to extend your lease.

Most landlords require you to pay up front the first month's rent, the last month's rent, and a security deposit. For example, if the rent on your apartment is $1,200 a month, you will have to pay $3,600 before you move in ($1,200 for the first month, $1,200 for the last month, and $1,200 for the security deposit). The last month's rent is to prevent you from moving out without giving the required notice first. The security deposit is in case you damage the apartment and the landlord has to make repairs after you leave. As long as you

When the time comes to move out on your own, your first home is likely to be an apartment that you rent.

take good care of the apartment, your security deposit should be returned to you in full within a specified time after you leave.

Your lease will also spell out what services are included in your rent (heat, water, trash removal, and so forth); whether you can have pets (fish, birds, and reptiles are usually allowed, dogs and cats maybe not); and where you can park. Each lease can be different depending on the landlord. Be sure to read it carefully—it is your responsibility to completely understand its terms. What your landlord tells you verbally does not matter. The only terms that matter are those included in the lease that you sign. Once you put your autograph on the dotted line, you are committed to following through.

Paying Taxes

Just about everyone complains at some point or other about paying taxes. That doesn't negate the fact that they are a necessary part of living in a civilized society. Taxes collected by the government

Some teens are surprised to find out they have to file a tax return because of their part-time job. "I had no idea I had to file my taxes until a friend mentioned it when we got our W-2 forms," says Madison Sero, a fifteen-year-old retail employee. "It's pretty intimidating. I don't know where to start."

Start by looking at the W-2 form your employer gave you. If you made more than $6,300, you are required to file a tax return.

Even if you earned under $6,300, you may still want to file. Helena Swyter, a certified public accountant and owner of Sweeter CPA, explains, "Say you earned $6,000 from a part-time job and had state and federal withholdings on your income. You may qualify to get some of that back so it would be worth filing, even though your income was below the cut-off."

Sero completed her tax forms and, to her surprise, received over $200 back from her part-time retail job. "It was so much easier than I thought, and I feel like I could do this all on my own next year," she says.

Quoted in Michelle Argento, "Let's Get Legit About Teens and Taxes," Financial Avenue, March 2, 2017. https://fa.financialavenue.org.

pay for things such as the roads we drive on, clean air and water, public safety (police and fire), schools, and a whole lot more. There are three kinds of taxes that people pay to the government: income taxes, sales taxes, and property taxes. Some of these taxes vary by state and even by county or city.

When government at any level (federal, state, and local) withholds a portion of every dollar you earn from your paycheck, it's called an income tax. The federal government, for example, taxes employees in three categories: federal income tax, Social Security, and Medicare. How much is withheld depends on how much money you make.

In general, the federal government has a graduated income tax system whereby the more you make, the higher percentage of tax you pay. However, the government allows people to subtract some expenses from their income—things like mortgage interest, medical expenses, and charitable donations—to lower their tax bill. These are called deductions.

Each year, usually by April 15, individuals must file their income tax return with the federal government. The return includes how much money you earned, how many deductions you are entitled to, and how much tax is due. If the government withheld more tax from your paycheck than is due, then you get a refund. But if you didn't pay enough, you will be required to pay the difference to the federal government.

Most states also impose an income tax as a percentage of your pay. States also allow some deductions, but fewer than the federal government. Like the federal government's, state tax returns are usually due by April 15. You could also get a refund or owe more tax, depending on your circumstances.

Finally, some local governments—the city, township, county, borough, or parish you live in—impose an earned income tax to pay for services, most notably public schools. Like the federal and state governments, an annual return is due to make sure you paid the right amount of tax.

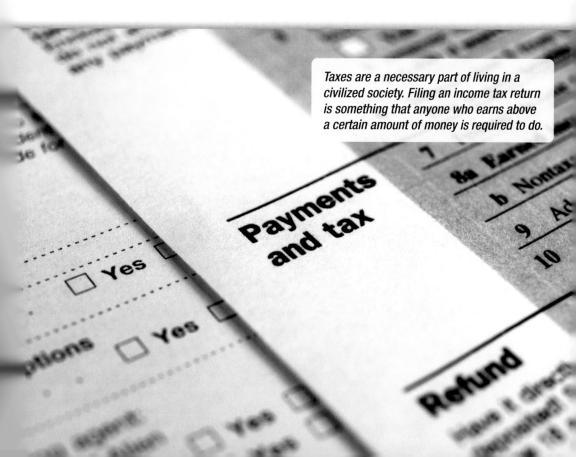

Taxes are a necessary part of living in a civilized society. Filing an income tax return is something that anyone who earns above a certain amount of money is required to do.

The goal for you should be to have the right amount of taxes withheld from your paycheck so that you don't get a refund or owe more tax. Some people look at a tax refund as free money. However, it is your money that you let the government hold, like an interest-free loan, for almost a year.

Another type of tax is sales tax. Depending on what you buy and where you buy it, some levels of government charge a tax as a percentage of the purchase price. For example, if you buy something for $100 and the sales tax is 6 percent, you'll pay a total of $106. Some items the government considers necessities, like food and medicine, are exempt from the sales tax. But other things, like video games, are included.

The third type of tax is called a property tax. People who own houses, buildings, and land pay a tax on them. It's usually imposed by a school district, a municipality (city, township, borough), and/or the county that the property is in. Each property

Building an Emergency Fund

Unexpected expenses happen to everyone. Whether it's a medical emergency, a job loss, or a car repair, you might be forced to dip into your savings or carry a balance on your credit card—both of which can lead to getting trapped in a cycle of debt and unpaid bills. "One of the first steps in climbing out of debt is to give yourself a way not to go further into debt," says NerdWallet columnist Liz Weston.

Financial experts recommend creating an emergency fund for unexpected expenses. This should be enough money to cover three to six months' worth of expenses. If your monthly living expenses total $2,000, that means you should have at least $6,000 stashed in a savings account.

When you create a personal budget, designate your emergency savings as one of your financial goals, and start saving as much as you can each month. If you unexpectedly find yourself with extra cash (say, from a large tax refund), your emergency fund might be the best place to put it. An emergency fund is something you want to set up ASAP, since the whole point is to be prepared for a large expense that might occur in the short term.

Quoted in Margarette Burnett, "Emergency Fund: What Is It and Why It Matters," NerdWallet, December 9, 2020. www.nerdwallet.com.

Buying car insurance is important because it protects you by covering the cost of repairing your vehicle if you have an accident.

is assigned an assessed value (how much it is worth), and the property tax is calculated based on the rate imposed by the municipality or county.

Insurance

Buying insurance is a way of protecting you against unexpected expenses. You pay a premium to an insurance company (monthly or annually), and they agree to pay for repairs if a covered item is damaged or if you get sick and need medical care. You can buy insurance for just about anything, but car insurance and health insurance are the two that will most likely affect you soonest.

Every car insurance policy includes a list of conditions that must be met

premium

The amount of money paid either monthly, quarterly, or annually for insurance coverage before the company will pay for a claim. So if you wreck your car doing doughnuts in the supermarket parking lot, there's a pretty good chance the insurance company is going to reject your claim for repairs.

Most policies also include a deductible that you must pay before the insurance company covers a claim. So let's say you slide off the road in a snowstorm and wreck your car, and it will cost $5,000 to make repairs. If you have a $1,000 deductible, your insurance company will pay $4,000 toward the bill. The rest is on you. The good news is that the higher the deductible, the lower your insurance premium.

Health insurance is much more complicated, with deductibles, copays, coinsurance, network providers, HMOs, PPOs, and more. Many employers provide some level of health insurance, but you will most likely have to pay a share of the premium. The good news is, for now, you can stay on your parents' health insurance plan until you are twenty-six.

Becoming an adult is an exciting time. But it also comes with a number of responsibilities, many of them related to money. Being prepared to manage your finances the right way as you enter the workforce, choose a place to live, and perhaps eventually start a family will go a long way toward giving you peace of mind to enjoy life.

Chapter Five

Investing in Your Future

The future, as most everyone realizes, is full of unknowns. But when it comes to finances, there are actually a few certainties. The power of compound growth is one of them. To understand what this means, let's begin with a question. Would you rather get exactly $10,000 every day for thirty days or receive a penny on day one and double that amount every day for thirty days?

Without giving it much thought, most people would choose the first option. But the more lucrative option is actually option two. You would have $300,000, not a bad haul, at the end of the thirty days if you chose the first option, but the second option would produce a sweet $5 million or so. The reason for this difference is compound growth, which is at the heart of every successful investing strategy. When you add the value of interest to the power of compound growth, you really come up with a powerful tool: compound interest.

Albert Einstein once called compound interest the eighth wonder of the world, because it seems to possess magical powers, like turning a penny into $5 million. According to Morningstar Investing Classroom, "Compound interest can help you achieve your financial goals, such as becoming a millionaire, retiring comfortably, or being financially independent. In order to use the compound interest most effectively, you should start investing early, invest as much as possible, and attempt to earn a reasonable rate of return."[21]

The Difference Between Saving and Investing

Saving money is the first step in investing. The next step is to make that hard-earned money work harder for you by investing it wisely in stocks, bonds, and mutual funds to prepare for life after work—otherwise known as retirement.

Steve Burkholder, author of *I Want More Pizza*, says that while retirement is a long way away for a teenager, it's important to think about it early. "Accumulating the amount of money you'll need for retirement takes time," says Burkholder. "In fact, for most, it takes a lifetime. Many people think they'll start later and catch up, but when the time comes they discover it's not possible to do so and they have to work later in life."[22]

While the terms *saving* and *investing* are often used inter-changeably, the website Smart About Money explains the difference this way:

- **Saving** is setting aside money you don't spend now for emergencies or for a future purchase. It's money you want to be able to access quickly, with little or no risk, and with the least amount of taxes. Financial institutions offer a number of different savings options.

- **Investing** is buying assets such as stocks, bonds, mu-tual funds or real estate with the expectation that your investment will make money for you. Investments usually are selected to achieve long-term goals.[23]

While investments are riskier than savings, they can also offer greater opportunity for rewards. The risk with investing is that you can lose all or part of your original investment. The reward is that if your investment does well, you stand to gain a lot more than you would in a savings account.

Another difference between saving and investing in terms of safety is that bank accounts are federally insured up to certain amounts, while investments are not. That means you can get your money back if a bank goes out of business. But if your investment tanks, you're out of luck.

One strategy that investment advisers offer to their clients is to diversify their investment portfolio to minimize losses. That means having a blend of investments, some that carry more risk but a potential for higher return and some that offer lower return but are more of a sure thing.

Another wise piece of advice for investors is to be patient. Investments often go up and down depending on what is happening in the economy. You can make a lot of money one day and lose as much, if not more, the next day. The key, say advisers, is to stay steady and focused on long-term investment goals.

portfolio

A collection of investments, mostly stocks and bonds, put together with a specific investment goal in mind

The Stock Market

One of the most popular ways people invest their money is in the stock market. When you buy stock in a corporation, you buy a certain number of shares—and each share represents a small part of the corporation. In other words, you are a part owner of that corporation. The size of your ownership depends on how many shares you own.

A company sells its stock to raise money. But it does not promise to pay you back, which is where the risk comes in. If the company does well and makes a profit, it may share that with you by paying you a monthly or yearly dividend. But that's just one way you can make money with stock ownership. The other way to make money

dividend

An amount of money paid to an investor depending on how much profit the investment makes

47

appreciation

How much an investment gains value over a period of time; the positive difference between what the investment cost and what it is worth at a particular time

is by selling the stock for a price that's higher than you paid. That's called appreciation.

But if the price of the stock goes down because the company does not do well, you risk losing all or part of the money you invested. As you may read in some advertisements, past performance is no indication of future results. That means that just because a stock did well in the past, there's no guarantee it will do well in the future.

There are several ways to invest in stock. Typically, you can purchase stock through an online retail brokerage. You can also work with an individual adviser who will guide you through the process and help you pick stocks to meet your goals. Various apps also provide a convenient platform for participating in the stock market.

Investing money that you have earned and keeping track of those investments is important. Various computer applications make the process of investing simple and convenient.

There are benefits to getting an early start on investing. Echo Huang, founder and president of Echo Wealth Management, presents a fictional scenario involving two young investors to illustrate the benefits. She calls them Lily and Anna—and both have their sights set on becoming millionaires someday.

Let's say Lily put $2,000 per year into the market from age twenty-four to thirty, on which she earned a 12 percent after-tax return and continued to earn 12 percent per year until she retired at age sixty-five. Anna also put in $2,000 per year and earned the same return but waited until she was thirty to start, and she continued to invest $2,000 per year until she retired at age sixty-five.

In the end, both would end up with about $1 million. However, Lily had to invest only $12,000 ($2,000 for six years), while Anna had to invest $72,000 ($2,000 for thirty-six years), or six times the amount that Lily invested, just for waiting only six years to start investing. Compounding can work magic when you have more time.

Quoted in Echo Wealth Management, "10 Money Management Tips for Teens," March 29, 2018. www.echowealth management.com.

Stocks are a good choice if you don't plan to touch your investment for a long time. The stock market sometimes has wild swings up or down depending on economic conditions around the world. But in the long run, stocks have proved to be a good investment. For example, if you had purchased one share of Apple stock for $22 when it was first offered in December 1980, your investment was worth about $15,000 in February 2021. If you had invested $100 (about four and a half shares at the time), it would be worth about $65,000 now. Of course, that doesn't mean anything until you actually sell the stock.

What Are Bonds?

When you buy bonds as an investment, you are basically lending the amount you pay to the bond issuer, which can be either a private company or a government agency. The government issuing bonds can be a municipality, a city, a state, or even the federal government. For example, you have probably heard of bonds issued by cities or states to raise money for education

Jully-Alma Taveras, founder of Investing Latina, says she didn't have a clear plan when she first started investing. "But a couple years into investing, I started to think more about what my retirement would look like and what my needs would be," she says.

Taveras started out by contributing $50 a month to her retirement account. As she started to make more money, with a new job or a raise, she increased the contribution. "I started to realize that I was investing with a purpose," she says.

For Taveras, that means financial stability while she is working and a goal to save $1 million by the time she retires. Today she is able to contribute at least $500 a month to her retirement account. "As I watched my contributions grow, the best part has been seeing the earnings from those investments," she says.

Quoted in Acorns, "I Started Investing $50 a Month When I was 19; Now I'm Working Toward Saving $1 Million," January 22, 2021. https://grow.acorns.com.

(school bonds), construction (maybe a sports arena), or some other community project.

The borrower (the bond issuer) promises to pay you back the money you lent it by a certain date and to give you a specific rate of interest as part of the repayments. Government bonds are typically a very low-risk investment, and the returns are generally low as well. You are exchanging safety for a relatively low rate of return.

Here's how a bond typically works: the investor (you) lends the issuer (the borrower) a certain amount of money, let's say $1,000. Each bond has a rate of interest it pays for a certain number of years. Let's say the bond you buy pays 5 percent a year for ten years. Each year, you will get a check for $50, for a total of $500. At the end of ten years, you will be able to return the bond for the original $1,000 you paid. Your total profit was $500.

Mutual Funds

Mutual funds are collections of stocks or bonds (or a combination of the two) that are funded by a large pool of investors. You can buy mutual funds with a specific goal in mind, such as high growth or maximum safety. But you still need to do your homework and choose mutual funds carefully, since performance varies from fund to fund.

Index mutual funds can be a good choice for young, first-time investors because they aim to mirror overall market returns and are measured by a specific index. For example, a Standard & Poor's (S&P) index fund may invest in the five hundred or so stocks that are included in the S&P 500. This means that when you buy shares in the fund, you are actually investing a little bit of money in each of those five hundred companies. If one or two of the companies do badly, you won't feel much of an effect on your investment. Index funds generally have very low fees.

Social Security and Pensions

There are two other ways you can save for retirement. One is Social Security, a program provided by the federal government, while the other is a pension offered by your employer.

Social Security is a federal government program designed to pay retired workers age sixty-five or older a continuing income after retirement. It is funded by a tax that is paid by both you (as long as you are working) and your employer. In 2021 the amount was 6.2 percent of your pay; your employer pays the same amount. If you make $100 a week, you each pay $6.20. All that money is sent to the federal government and credited to your Social Security account.

When you reach retirement age—it varies, depending on what year you were born—you are eligible to begin collecting monthly payments from Social Security. According to the Social Security Administration, the average Social Security benefit was $1,543 in January 2021. The maximum possible Social Security benefit for someone who retires at full retirement age was $3,011 in 2021.

Some employers—mostly government agencies and school districts—offer a defined benefit pension plan. This means an employer promises to give its retired employee a certain amount of money every month, with the amount determined by how much money the employee earned while working and the number of years he or she worked. For example, under a defined benefit pension plan, an employee who earned $50,000 a year and worked for thirty years might receive $1,000 a month for the rest of his or her life. While employees did not contribute to the pension plan, they did not have any control over how much it paid out. That amount was decided by the employer.

But with people living longer and collecting pensions for more years than expected, many companies came to realize that a defined benefit pension plan was not sustainable, so they began to offer defined contribution plans. These are known as 401(k) plans. These plans shift the responsibility for developing a sustainable retirement income from the employer to the employee. Today, the vast majority of employees participate in 401(k) accounts, to produce the income they need and want during retirement.

A 401(k) plan allows employees to contribute a set amount of money from each paycheck to a retirement account up to a

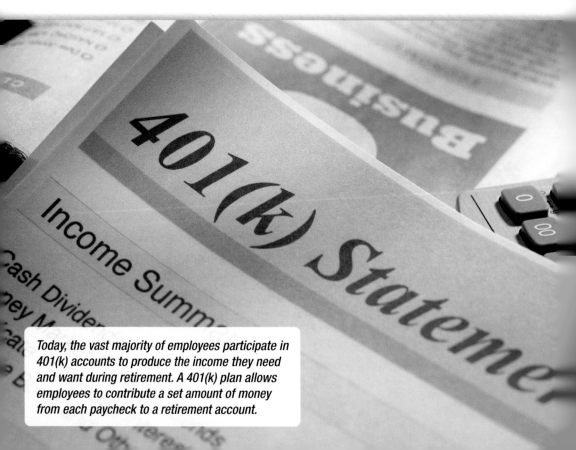

Today, the vast majority of employees participate in 401(k) accounts to produce the income they need and want during retirement. A 401(k) plan allows employees to contribute a set amount of money from each paycheck to a retirement account.

certain annual limit set by the Internal Revenue Service. There are two types of 401(k) plans: traditional and Roth. The difference is that traditional 401(k) plans are funded with pretax dollars and are taxed at ordinary rates when you begin withdrawals. Roth plans are funded with after-tax dollars but are not taxed when you begin to make withdrawals.

One big advantage to a 401(k) is that many employers match their employees' contributions—either dollar for dollar or a set portion. For example, if you choose to set aside 6 percent of your pay in a 401(k) account, your employer may also contribute 6 percent or some other amount.

401(k) plans are also self-directed, which means employees have a lot of control over how and where their money is invested from the selection of options offered by their employer's plan. Usually, it's a mix of stock mutual funds but can also include stock in their own company. Employees can manage their accounts online through whatever brokerage firm is handling the plan. One potential downside to a 401(k) is that you can't begin making withdrawals until you are fifty-nine and a half years old without paying a significant penalty under most circumstances.

Why Start Now?

As a teenager, you might be wondering whether it's worth learning about investing at such a young age. What's the point now, when you could be doing so much more fun, exciting things with your money? But as we've seen with the power of compounding, the sooner you start investing, the longer your money has to work for you. That's why experts say it's important to learn the basics of investing at a young age.

Source Notes

Introduction: Why You Need to Be Financially Literate

1. "Teenage Money Management (Tips on Personal Finance for Teens)," Intuit *MintLife*, December 8, 2020. mint.intuit.com .Investopedia.
2. "U.S. National Strategy for Financial Literacy 2020," U.S. Financial Literacy and Education Commission, 2020. https:// home.treasury.gov.
3. Quoted in Kathryn Tuggle, "Teaching Gap: 83% of Teens Don't Know How to Manage Money," Fox Business, July 17, 2012. www.foxbusiness.com

Chapter One: Earn It, Save It, Spend It

4. Tracy Morgan, "The Pros and Cons of Teens Getting Jobs," *TeenLife Blog*, June 11, 2019. www.teenlife.com.
5. Rana Al-fayez, "Budgeting Basics for Students: The Ultimate Guide," FuturFund, October 8, 2020. http://futurfund.org.
6. Steve Burkholder, *I Want More Pizza*. Schenectady, NY: Overcome, 2017, p. 17.
7. Al-fayez, "Budgeting Basics for Students."
8. Echo Huang, "10 Money Management Tips for Teens," LinkedIn, March 29, 2018. www.linkedin.com.

Chapter Two: Taking on Debt

9. Dave Ramsey, "12 Reasons Why People Stay in Debt," Ramsey Solutions, September 30, 2020. www.daveramsey .com.
10. Alana Biden, "7 Things to Teach Your Teen About Credit Cards Before They Leave for College," GreatSchools, June 5, 2017. www.greatschools.org.
11. Beth Kobliner, *Make Your Kid a Money Genius (Even If You're Not)*. New York: Simon & Schuster, 2017.
12. Debbie Schwartz, "5 Important Credit Card Lessons for Teens and Young Adults," Sallie Mae, April 2, 2020. www .salliemae.com.
13. Schwartz, "5 Important Credit Card Lessons for Teens and Young Adults."

Chapter Three: Paying for College

14. Quoted in Teddy Nykiel and Anna Helhoski, "How to Pay for College: 8 Expert-Approved Tips," NerdWallet, August 28, 2019. www.nerdwallet.com.
15. Ken Clark, "The Basics of College Tuition, Room, and Board," The Balance, June 22, 2020. www.thebalance.com.
16. Clark, "The Basics of College Tuition, Room, and Board."
17. Brandon Busteed, "The Convincing and Confusing Value of College Explained," *Forbes*, September 3, 2018. www.forbes.com.
18. Tyler Yates, "6 Easy Tips on How to Get a Scholarship for College," *Earnest* (blog), September 1, 2020. www.earnest.com.

Chapter Four: Living on Your Own

19. Valencia Higuera, "Moving Out of Your Parents' House—6 Financial Tips to Live on Your Own," Money Crashers, 2021. www.moneycrashers.com.
20. Alecia Pirulis, "How to Rent Your First Apartment," Apartments.com, January 18, 2019. www.apartments.com.

Chapter Five: Investing in Your Future

21. "The Magic of Compounding," Morningstar Interactive Classroom, 2015. https://news.morningstar.com.
22. Burkholder, *I Want More Pizza*, p. 28.
23. "The Difference Between Saving and Investing," Smart About Money. www.smartaboutmoney.org.

For More Information

Books

Steve Burkholder, *I Want More Pizza*. Schenectady, NY: Overcome, 2017.

Terri Dougherty, *Building a Budget and Savings Plan*. San Diego, CA: ReferencePoint, 2021.

Stuart A. Kallen, *Managing Credit and Debt*. San Diego, CA: ReferencePoint, 2021.

Ramit Sethi, *I Will Teach You to Be Rich*. New York: Workman, 2019.

Cary Siegel, *Why Didn't They Teach Me This in School, Too?* Simple Strategic Solutions, 2018. Kindle.

Bola Sokunbi, *Clever Finance Girl.* Hoboken, NJ: Wiley, 2019.

Michael Zisa, *The Early Investor: How Teens and Young Adults Can Become Wealthy*. North Charleston, SC: CreateSpace Independent Publishing Platform, 2020. Kindle.

Websites

Investopedia (www.investopedia.com). This is a comprehensive website that covers all aspects of investing. It includes "Investing 101: A Tutorial for Beginner Investors" that will help new investors, including teenagers, navigate the complicated stock market.

MyMoney (www.mymoney.gov). This website provides a variety of resources for teens, with links to games, financial resources, tax information, and money-saving tips.

Teens Guide to Money (www.teensguidetomoney.com). This website is a great source for financial tips and information aimed specifically at teenagers, from building a résumé to getting tips on smart shopping and advice for wise investing.

TheMint (www.themint.org). One of the best sites for all ages, TheMint provides financial management information for kids, teens, parents, and teachers. Sections for teens include tips for earning, saving, spending, investing, and safeguarding their money.

Apps, Games, and Online Tools

Financial Football (http://practicalmoneyskills.com/play/financial_ football). Visa has teamed up with the National Football League to produce this fast-paced, interactive game that teaches financial skills. The latest version features 3-D graphics and advanced football plays.

Honey (www.addhoney.com). With this free app, when you shop online, Honey searches for and applies the best discount code for your purchases.

Moneytopia (www.saveandinvest.org/moneytopia). In this game, you keep track of finances with the ultimate goal of successfully managing your money throughout life, until you achieve your Big Dream.

Savings Calculator (https://tools.finra.org/savings_calculator). Use this handy financial calculator to determine the amount to save to reach your savings goal.

Index

Picture Credits

Joe Ferry is a veteran journalist who has worked as a newspaper reporter and editor, as well as a public relations and marketing consultant. He lives in Montgomery County, Pennsylvania.